ART NOUVEAU

ABSTRACT DESIGNS

Stemmer House
PUBLISHERS, INC.
2627 Caves Road
Owings Mills, MD 21117

REBECCA McKILLIP

Inquiries should be directed to
Stemmer House Publishers, Inc.
2627 Caves Road
Owings Mills, Maryland 21117

A Barbara Holdridge book
Printed and bound in the United States of America

First printing 1983
Second printing 1989

Introduction

Anyone who loves long sinuous lines, elegant ornament and graceful forms will find pleasure in recognizing a poster, a piece of furniture or a bit of jewelry as an example of the Art Nouveau style. The innocent sensuality of a Mucha girl, the ornate, over-refined decadence of the elegant salons in a Beardsley illustration, the cool glowing colors of a Tiffany stained-glass window have a timeless grace and beauty which delight art lovers now even as it did almost a hundred years ago when the style flourished.

The artistic style known as Art Nouveau developed in the latter part of the nineteenth century and flourished between about 1880 and 1905. It was not one broad movement which began in one artistic center and then spread from country to country, from imitator to imitator. Rather, this artistic movement developed almost simultaneously across Europe, Great Britain and America as a result of very similar conditions in the political and artistic worlds. Each movement had very specific individual characteristics and was called by a different name. In Germany it was called *Jugendstil;* in France, *Style Moderne;* in Austria, *Sezsionstil;* in America, *Tiffany Style;* in Italy, *Stile Liberty* or *Stile Nuovo;* and in Spain, *Modernismo* or *Style Gaudi.* The term *L'Art Nouveau* was taken from the name of a shop in Paris, where in 1895 there was held a "Salon de l'Art Nouveau" featuring the work of Louis Comfort Tiffany, Henri de Toulouse-Lautrec, Pierre Bonnard, Eugène Grasset and Aubrey Beardsley. Now generally accepted as the name of the international style, "art nouveau" was indeed a new kind of art which put an end to the old artistic precepts of the early nineteenth century and which paved the way for the art of the modern age in the twentieth century.

Historical Background

In the world of the late nineteenth century, Western society was reeling from the profound changes worked upon its political and social life by the immense technological developments of the Industrial Revolution. It was a time of confusion and upheaval in the established socio-political order, a time for reevaluation of long-upheld traditions. The newly important middle class was beginning to assert itself as an economic and social force, and consequently as a determining voice of the fashions, tastes and mores of the day. Even as the middle class became increasingly more influential and established as a social entity, traditionalists sought to preserve the conditions of the pre-industrial world by retaining all of the old classical ideals.

In the art world, this tenacious death grip on the traditions of the past, or "historicism," attempted to preserve the classical mode of artistic expression at all costs, as well as to stifle any attempt at novelty or variety. The resulting work of this traditional ideal was manneristic, over-refined and stagnant; yet because of its "classical" intent, the historicists considered even the worst of its examples acceptable and preferable to anything which introduced creative innovation.

In the 1880s and 90s another artistic movement, whose objective it was to resist the changes brought about by the Industrial Revolution, arose in England.

Inspired by the writing of the popular art critic John Ruskin, the architect William Morris advocated the remastery of handicrafts by reviving the crafts guilds of the middle ages. Ruskin wrote that it was only through a study of nature, of botany and geology, that the artist could master the principles of organization and form. Furthermore, art could have no character without human touch; it is the morality and the ideals of the artist, not the impersonal precision of the machine, which gives beauty to design. The Arts and Crafts movement, led by Morris, opposed the heavy, ugly machine-made goods which were being turned out in enormous quantities to satisfy the demands of the new, moneyed middle class. Followers of the movement tried to create an object of beauty and moral value through good design and expert craftsmanship. The movement was limited, however, by its impracticality and its refusal to recognize the inevitability of the machine age.

The Art Nouveau style developed on the Continent at about the same time as the Arts and Crafts movement in England. Promoters of the new style shared with the followers of Arts and Crafts the same distaste for the stale traditional art of the historicists, and the same opposition to the bad design produced by industrialization. In contrast, however, proponents of the Art Nouveau style more realistically sought to create designs which might exploit the artistic potential of the machine. At this time, many young painters were forced to turn to the minor arts and commerical design in order to make a living, while struggling to have their paintings accepted in the exclusive yearly Parisian exhibitions. The poor quality of the existing design work in the decorative arts and advertising challenged the young artists, and so in poster design, book illustration, and furniture, textile and jewelry design, they found an outlet for their talents and their powers of creativity and innovation which did not find acceptance in the Paris Salon. All over Europe young artists formed into groups to work in the new style, in rebellious opposition to the now stale traditional approach to art. That the world had been starving for new artistic thought was made clear by the rapidity with which the movement spread and by the vitality with which it was adopted and developed.

Along with its distinctive innovation and beauty, Art Nouveau was also responsible for a change in the condescending attitude that the decorative arts were insignificant in the realm of artistic expression. The line separating fine art from its poorer relations of interior decoration, illustration, and commerical design was blurred; hence, the influence of Art Nouveau can be seen in such twentieth-century modern movements as Bauhaus, Surrealism and abstract art.

Style and Expression

Art Nouveau was the last style which embraced all fields of artistic activity. In addition to its influence on painting, Art Nouveau design found expression in architecture and in interior decoration—especially in bathroom and stairway decoration and in locks and fasteners, wallpaper, carpeting, tapestries, furniture, glass and ceramics. Interior decorators cleared the drawing room's confusion of Victorian clutter and, with the unity of purpose advocated by English architect A.W.N. Pugin, designed rooms whose every line and ornament was in complete harmony. One architect-decorator went so far as to design for his wife dresses and jewelry which were coordinated with the decor of the rooms in which she would be entertaining.

Book illustration, typography, graphics and poster design all flourished in the Art Nouveau style. Some of the most notable and well-known are illustrations such as Aubrey Beardsley's "The Rape of the Lock" and posters by Alphonse Mucha and Henri de Toulouse-Lautrec. Each country had its periodical devoted to this fresh approach to art and design. Publications like *The Studio* in London and *Pan* and *Jugend* in Germany were invaluable sources of information and inspiration to artists. These periodicals were also responsible for public acceptance of the style, and for bringing artists such as England's Beardsley and Walter Crane, America's William Bradley and Austria's Kolomon Moser and Gustav Klimt to the public eye.

Although each country or artistic center developed the new style in its own distinct way, there were certain stylistic characteristics common to all. The style is based on natural elements, a legacy of the writings of Ruskin and Pugin and the premise of the Arts and Crafts movement. Vegetation, marine life and landscapes were studied and then conventionalized to suit the decorative scheme. The emphasis of the design is on its decorative conception and treatment. Ornament is rendered perfectly, to the smallest detail. The nature and purpose of the object and its decoration had to be in complete harmony, as did all elements within the composition of the design. The weights of black and white space are perfectly counter-balanced.

Art Nouveau is essentially a linear style, most easily recognized by its sinuous, flowing "whiplash line." The curve of this line takes on the chief expressive role in Art Nouveau. Its undulating swirls and coils create a sense of movement in the heavily ornamented design. Representation of objects and people is greatly stylized. The female figure is one of the most frequently used motifs, and it is conventionalized in the same way as the natural elements of the decoration. The stylized flowing line of the woman's dress and hair and her languorous pose make her one with the rhythmic pattern of the flowers which surround her.

With the abundance of ornamentation and the linear orientation, the impact of Art Nouveau design is emphatically graphic. Every object in the design is surrounded by a heavy black outline, so that all elements are flattened and brought into the same surface plane. The illusion of depth is destroyed in favor of an emphasis on the mosaic-like pattern of the design.

Although Art Nouveau's graphic nature makes its exclusively black and white designs among the most striking examples of the style, the tints also characteristic of the Art Nouveau are quite beautiful and distinctive as well. Bright colors are rarely seen. Instead, pastel shades of grey, green, red, blue, violet, mauve and pink, together with a chalky white, make up the delicate palette with which the black outline contrasts so dramatically.

As a transitional movement, the Art Nouveau style did much for artistic thought in the late nineteenth century—an exhilarating liberation from the weary historical tradition of the early part of the century. It inspired fresh respect for the applied arts of interior decoration and furniture design, and for the commerical arts of both illustration and poster design. The newly acquired dignity of the minor arts provided a link with the fine arts. The artists brought a spirit of social commitment and moral obligation to their work, which was felt in the social and political worlds.

As an innovative style, Art Nouveau introduced new thought which paved the way for the "modern art" of the twentieth century. Finally, on an aesthetic level, the movement produced many magnificent artistic treasures, in the work of such artists as Tiffany, Mucha, Lalique and Beardsley. The Art Nouveau style continues to bring delight to art lovers and inspiration to artists and designers of this modern age.

R. McK.

FOR MY MOTHER

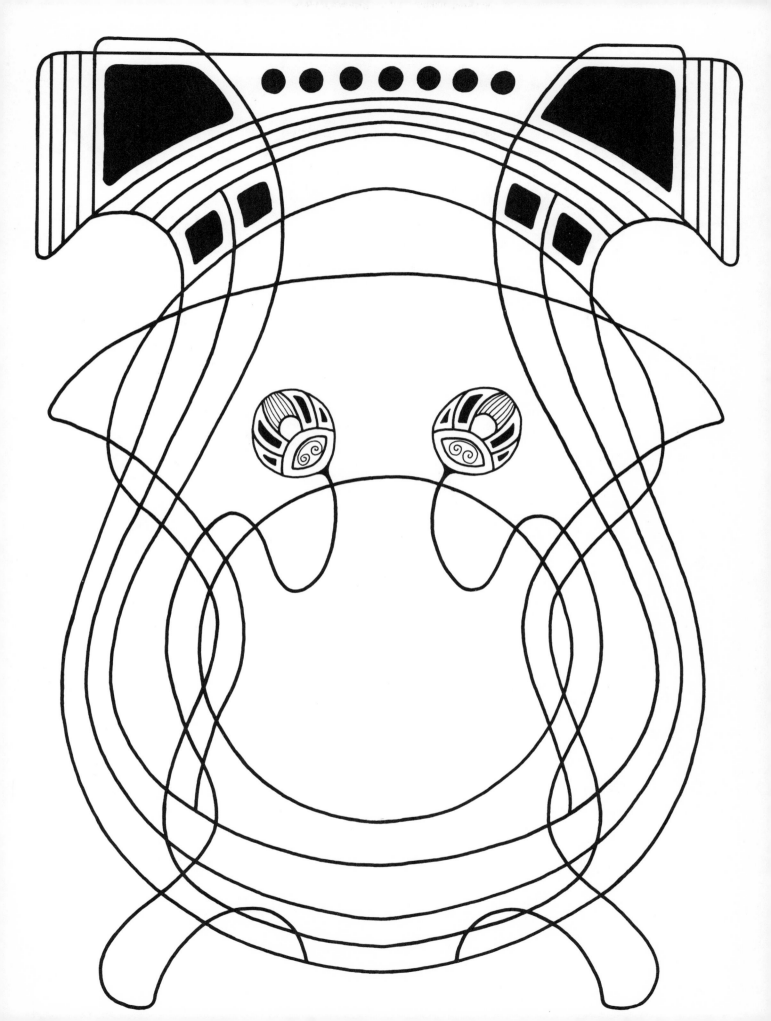

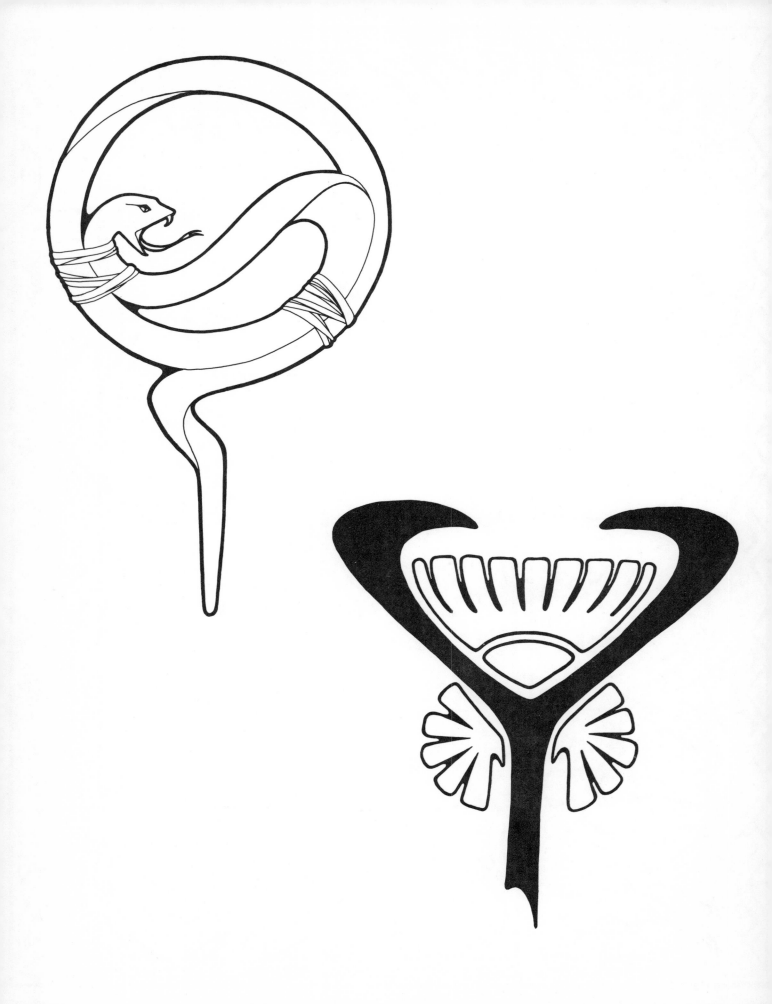

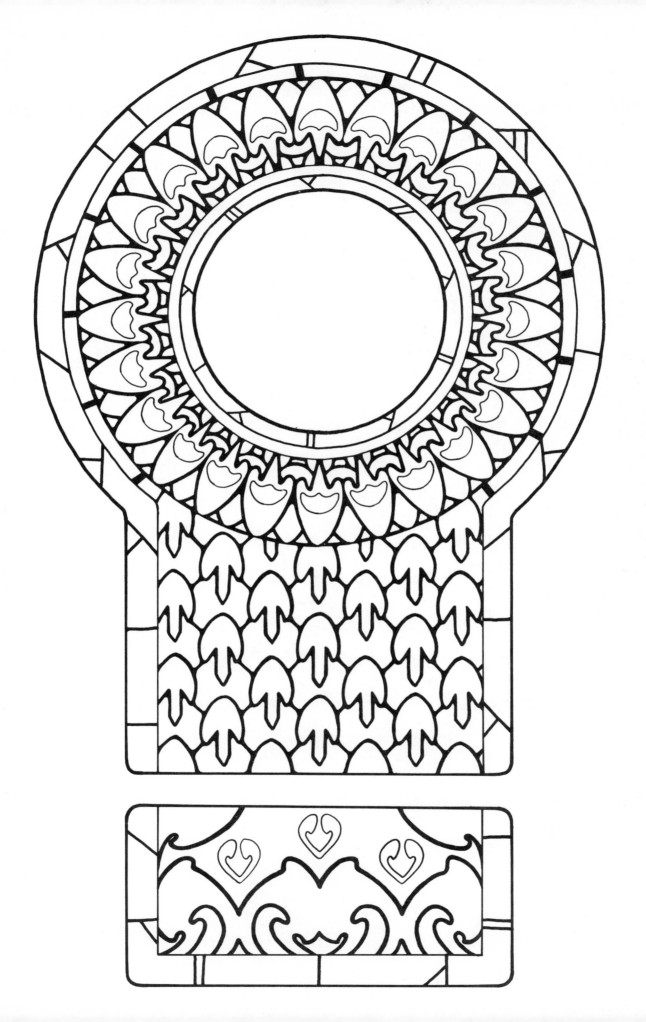

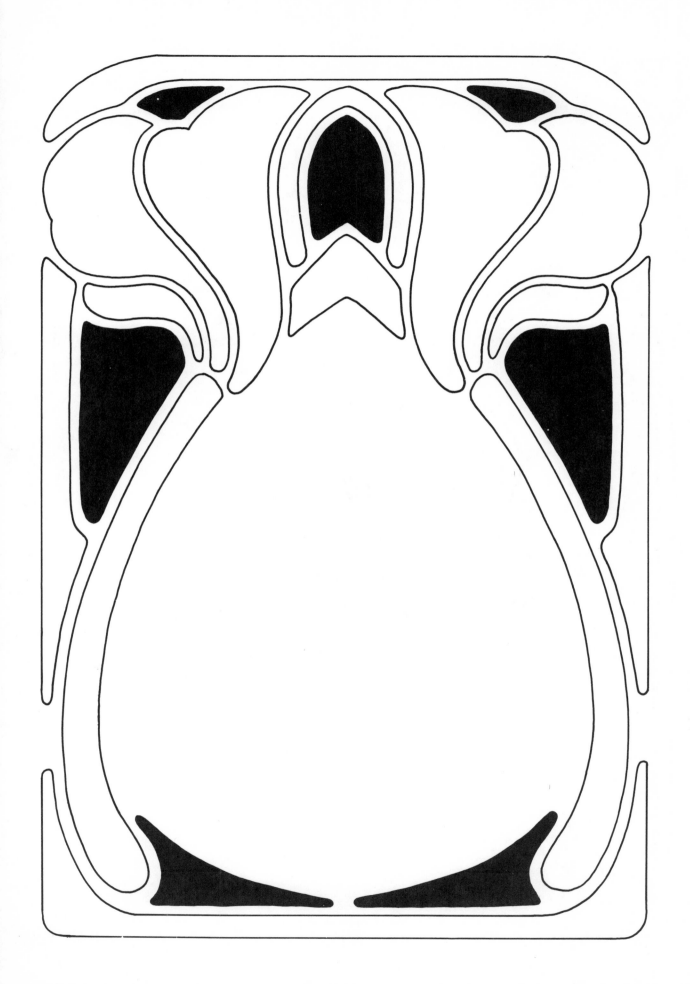

Colophon
Designed by Barbara Holdridge
Composed in Times Roman by Brown Composition, Baltimore, Maryland, with calligraphic initials and title by Keith McConnell

Printed on 75-pound Williamsburg Offset and bound by St. Mary's Press, Hollywood, Maryland